Celebrating
Friendship

Other Women of Faith Bible Studies

Discovering Your Spiritual Gifts
Embracing Forgiveness
Experiencing God's Presence
Finding Joy
Growing in Prayer
Knowing God's Will
Strengthening Your Faith

WOMEN OF FAITH℠
BIBLE STUDY SERIES

Celebrating
Friendship

Written by

JUDITH COUCHMAN

General Editor

TRACI MULLINS

ZondervanPublishingHouse
Grand Rapids, Michigan

A Division of HarperCollins*Publishers*

For Andy Landis,
a truly remarkable friend

Acknowledgments

Many thanks to Mary McNeil, Traci Mullins, and Ann Spangler for bringing their ideas and editorial expertise to this Bible study. And as always, I'm grateful to those who prayed: Charette Barta, Opal Couchman, Win Couchman, Madalene Harns, Karen Hilt, Shirley Honeywell, and Nancy Lemons. Their love and friendship inspired the ideas in these pages.

Celebrating Friendship
Copyright © 1998 by Women of Faith, Inc.

Requests for information should be addressed to:

ZondervanPublishingHouse
Grand Rapids, Michigan 49530

ISBN: 0-310-21338-X

General Editor, Traci Mullins
Cover and interior illustration by Jim Dryden
Interior design by Sue Vandenberg Koppenol

Printed in the United States of America

CONTENTS

FOREWORD

The best advice I ever received was in 1955. I was twenty-three. Somebody had the good sense to say to me, "Luci, if you want to give yourself a gift, learn all you can about the Bible. Start going to a Bible class and don't stop until you have some knowledge under your belt. You won't be sorry." Having just graduated from college, I was living with my parents, and together we drove more than twenty miles to attend that class. We went four nights a week for two years. I've *never* been sorry.

Nothing I've ever done or learned has meant more to me than those classes. Unless I was on my deathbed, I didn't miss. I went faithfully, took notes, absorbed everything like a sponge, asked questions relentlessly, and loved *every* minute! (I probably drove the teacher crazy.)

Today, more than forty years later, this wonderful storehouse of truth is my standard for living, giving, loving, and learning. It is my Rock and Fortress, the pattern for enjoying abundant life on earth, and for all eternity. I know what I believe, and why. I'm open to change on my tastes, personal opinions, even some of my choices. But change my biblical convictions? No way! They're solid and secure, based on God's inerrant, enduring, and unchanging Word. There's nothing like learning God's truth. As he says, it sets you free.

Women of Faith Bible studies are designed to help you deal with everyday problems and issues concerning you. Experienced and wise women who, like the rest of us, want to know God intimately, have written these lessons. They encourage us to dig into the Scriptures, read them carefully, and respond to thought-provoking questions. We're invited to memorize certain verses as sources of support and guidance, to hide his Word in our heads and hearts.

7

The clever ideas in these studies make me smile. The stories move my spirit. There are valuable suggestions in dealing with others, quotations that cause me to stop and think. The purpose of every activity is to put "some knowledge under your belt" about the Bible and its relevance for life *this very day.*

Give yourself a gift. Grab your Bible, a pencil, notepad, cup of coffee . . . maybe even a friend . . . and get started. I assure you—you'll *never* be sorry.

LUCI SWINDOLL

HOW TO USE THIS GUIDE

Women of Faith Bible studies are designed to take you on a journey toward a more intimate relationship with Christ by bringing you together with your sisters in the faith. We all want to continue to grow in our Christian lives, to please God, to be a vital part of our families, churches, and communities. But too many of us have tried to grow alone. We haven't found enough places where we feel safe to share our heartaches and joys and hopes. We haven't known how to support and be supported by other women in ways that really make a difference. Perhaps we haven't had the tools.

The guide you are about to use will give you the tools you need to explore a fundamental aspect of your walk with God *with* other women who want to grow, too. You'll not only delve into Scripture and consider its relevance to your everyday life, but you'll also get to know other women's questions, struggles, and victories—many similar, some quite different from your own. This guide will give you permission to be yourself, to share honestly, to care for one another's wounds, and laugh together when you take yourselves too seriously.

Each of the six lessons in this guide is divided into six sections. Most you'll discuss as a group; others you'll cover on your own during the week between meetings.

A Moment for Quiet Reflection. The questions in this section are meant to be answered in a few minutes of privacy sometime before you join your group each week. You may already carve out a regular time of personal reflection in your days, so you've experienced the refreshment and insight these times bring to your soul. However, if words like "quiet," "reflection," and "refreshment" have become unfamiliar to you, let this guide get you started with the invaluable practice of setting aside personal time to think, to rest, to pray. Sometimes the answers you write down to the questions in this section will be discussed as a group when you come together; other times they'll just give you something to ponder deep within. Don't neglect this important reflection time each week, and include enough time to read the introduction to the lesson so you'll be familiar with its focus.

Knowing God's Heart. The questions in this section will take you into the Bible, where you and the women in your group can discover God's heart and mind on the subject at hand. You'll do the Bible study together, reading the Scriptures aloud and sharing your understanding of the passage so all of you can learn together what God has to say about your own heart and life, right now. While you don't need to complete the study questions prior to each group session, it will be helpful for you to read through this part of the lesson beforehand so you can begin thinking about your answers. There is a lot to cover in each lesson, so being somewhat familiar with the content before your meetings will save your group time when you actually do your study together.

Friendship Boosters. A big part of why you've come together is to deepen your friendships with other women and to support each other in meaningful ways. The questions and activities in this section are designed to link you together in bonds of friendship, faith, and joy. Whether you are meeting the other women in your group for the first time or are old friends, this section will boost the quality and pleasure in your relationships as well as give you opportunities to support each other in practical ways.

Just for Fun. God's plan for our lives certainly isn't all work and no play! Central to being a woman of faith is cultivating a joyful spirit, a balanced perspective, and an ability to enjoy life because of God's faithfulness and sovereignty. Every week you'll be given an idea or activity that will encourage you to enjoy your journey, laugh, and lighten your load as you travel the path toward wholehearted devotion together.

Praying Together. Nothing is more important than asking God to help you and your friends as you learn how to live out his truths in your lives. Each time you get together you'll want to spend some time talking to him about your individual and mutual concerns.

Making It Real in Your Own Life. You'll respond to these questions or activities on your own after group meetings, but don't consider them just an afterthought. This section is critical because it will help you discover more ways to apply what you've learned and discussed to your own life in the days and weeks ahead. This section will be a key to making God's liberating truths more real to you personally.

In each section, space is provided after each question for you to record your answers, as well as thoughts stimulated by others' answers during group discussion. While you can gain wisdom from completing parts of this guide on your own, you'll miss out on a lot of the power—and the fun!—of making it a group experience.

One woman should be designated as the group facilitator, but she needn't have any training in leading a Bible study or discussion group. The facilitator will just make sure the discussion stays on track, and there are specific notes to help her in the "Leader's Guide" section at the back of this book. Keeping your group size to between four and eight participants is ideal because then it will be possible for everyone to share each week. The length of time you'll need to complete the lessons together will depend largely on how much the participants talk, so the group facilitator will need to monitor the time to keep it under ninety minutes. The facilitator can also speed up or slow down the group time by choosing to skip some discussion questions or concentrate longer on others. If you decide to do this study in a larger group or Sunday school class, split up into smaller groups for discussion. Especially make sure no one gets left out of the process of building friendships and having fun!

Now that you've studied the map, your journey should go smoothly. Celebrate being women of faith as you travel together. *Enjoy!*

May we not become so busy, harried, and overcommitted that we neglect that part of our soul that is fed and sustained by friendship.
MARILYN MEBERG

INTRODUCTION
You've Gotta Have Friends

This morning, while you took a shower, your preschooler painted a mural in the dining room (on your new, flowered wallpaper) with peanut butter and blueberry jam. Then your cranky eighth-grader overslept and missed his car pool. Returning home after a mad dash to the junior high, toddler in tow, you now boot up the computer. A message appears on the screen (it might as well be written in Greek, for all you know about this stuff) that blocks access to your company's files.

The phone rings. Your daughter forgot her lunch. Could you bring it to the front office at another school across town? While you're telling her to try begging or fasting for that meal, another call clicks in. It's your husband. He just got assigned a last-minute business trip. Could you pack his bags? (Nobody ever says *please*, anymore.) Almost precisely as you hang up the phone (oops! you forgot your daughter was holding on the other line), there's a *CRASH!* Your darling baby is at it again.

All this, and it's only nine o'clock.

Okay, so this didn't happen to you. But you recognize the *s-t-r-e-s-s* that leaks into your life, travels up your spine, and stiffens your neck with its relentless grip. In fact, with the kids, the job, the church, the husband (or ex), the neighbors, the finances, the relatives, the cleaning, the shopping, the everything else, you wonder if you're going to spin irrevocably out of control. Or when you'll ever take care of yourself.

Go to Starbucks and sip coffee with friends? You just can't afford to take the time.

But really, you can't afford not to.

Researchers say good friends contribute to your overall wellness. In other words, if you carve out time to nurture meaningful, listen-to-each-other friendships, you'll be happier and healthier—and you'll live longer, too. (You want to enjoy the years *after* the kids are gone, right?) The time spent chatting, lunching, playing, even weeping with friends meets needs that nothing else can. These spiritual sisters help you relax, replenish your soul, slough off the stress, gain perspective, and stay on track when you're about to derail. Or as Patsy Clairmont puts it, "Friendships are the ship the Lord often launches to keep my boat afloat."

Sounds good. But with everyone so busy, how do you make the connection?

That's what this small group discussion guide is about. Whether you're stressed-out, bored and lonely, looking for new friends, or scuttling to keep up with longtime soul mates, these six sessions will encourage your group to cultivate woman-to-woman friendships. You will:

- relate your friendship expectations;
- learn how to appreciate the similarities and differences among friends;
- discuss ways to be supportive, honest, and committed;
- find out how to work through relationship snags;
- celebrate joys and triumphs together.

Most of all, the springboard for this discussion will be God's Word. The Lord is the faithful Friend who sticks "closer than a brother" (or a sister!), and your group will explore his everlasting commitment to us, the friendship stories in his Book, and the qualities of his Spirit that deepen relationships. The God of the universe teaching you about friendship? There's no better expert!

So go ahead. Dig into the Bible. Talk and laugh and disagree. Have fun discovering, supporting, and challenging one another. Celebrate what you've learned and cry when you need to. Because that's what friendship is all about. And remember: For the sake of your health, the sake of your sanity, the sake of your soul, you've gotta have friends.

Wanted: A Few Good Women

W anted: *A few good women to form a circle of friends. Must be smart, fun-loving, always there when I need them. The type who'll love my kids, drop dinner by when I'm stressed, always see the best in me, and never complain about their lives or anything I do. Gift-givers and surprise-party throwers a plus. Required: A commitment to never change, move away, or like anybody else better than me.*

Wouldn't it be great if you could write a want ad for the perfect group of friends, and they'd show up at your door (with the exact characteristics you requested) to whisk you away for a Saturday adventure? It's a nice, lingering thought, but in the real world friendships don't develop that way. Yes, there are times you hit it off with someone immediately and the relationship easily flourishes. But most good friendships develop over the years, fluctuate up and down, and challenge you to grow. And, of course, there are friendships that blow up or fizzle out, leaving you to wonder, *What did I do wrong?*

However you gather up friendships, you have expectations about them. (Even if you consider yourself the easygoing type, when you dig inside, you'll find a friendship code lurking about—and what it says may surprise you!) The irony is, friends seldom express these desires (or demands) to each other. We make lists and ponder how to find Mr. Right, buy a new car, or assess a job offer. But friendship? We tend to enter that blindfolded. We don't know what we want or what the other person expects. We miss each other's signals and when the relationship falters, we're perplexed and disappointed.

But wait. Don't give up hope. Fabulous friendships are possible. They're fun, heartwarming, cherishable, and not-to-be-missed. And guess what? They thrive on respecting each other's expectations, even if they can't all be fulfilled.

So for this session, you get to dream a little. You'll answer the question, "What is a good friend like?" You have a chance to be honest about what matters and hoot about your way-out-there ideas. Then you'll see what the Bible says about friendship qualities, helping you define what good relationships can be. Because along with you, God wants the best for your friendships.

A friend is a gift you give yourself.
ROBERT LOUIS STEVENSON

A Moment
for Quiet Reflection

1. Squeeze out a few minutes alone, grab a pen and pad (or the computer), and make three off-the-top-of-your-head lists. To create the first list, answer the question, "Why do I need friendships?" For the second list, answer, "What is a good friend like?" In the third list, "What do I want from my friendships?" Don't censor yourself. Write as little or as much as comes to mind. Be honest, idealistic, even silly, to spill out your ideas.

2. Review your lists and ask, "Are my friendships living up to these expectations?" Circle the answer that applies:

Yes   Some are, some aren't   No   You've got to be kidding!

3. Give God a state-of-the-friendships report. Thank him for the great friends in your life. Ask him to heal the hurting relationships and remove any barriers you have to making new friends. Invite him to teach you how to nurture loving, lasting friendships.

Knowing God's Heart

The Bible brims with stories about friendship. Abraham and Jehovah. David and Jonathan. Naomi and Ruth. Daniel and his furnace friends. Mary and Elizabeth. Jesus and the disciples. Paul and Timothy. God's Word also offers advice on making friends and managing relationships.

In fact, most of the Book speaks to relationships. Companionship is God's intent for us, but he knows we're only human. Sometimes we need help sorting out our "stuff" and "behaving ourselves" in even the best of friendships. He wants us to throw out the junk and jump into the joy.

To get to the hugs and hilarity, though, we begin with understanding our expectations and how they affect friendships.

1. Get ready for some surprising insights and a few laughs. Referring to your own list, "What is a good friend like?" create a list as a group. Write the responses on a chalkboard, easel pad, or any place everyone can see it. Include the ridiculous ("a good friend doesn't hiss at my cat") to the sublime ("she never lies to me"), and don't pass judgment on anyone's ideas.

2. Now review the list, which by now probably staggers and describes Superwoman. Why do you think we have so many expectations about friends?

3. This will take grit, but as a group choose from the list the five to ten most important qualities of a friend. What does this short list reveal about the friendship needs you share in common?

4. Though the Bible's how-to advice mostly addresses relationships in general, it does make some direct statements about friends and friendship. Divide the following Scriptures among the group members and take turns reading them aloud. For each Scripture ask, "What is the friendship quality expressed here?" and write it on the chalkboard or easel pad under the title, God's List. Then consider, "Why is this quality important?"

- Proverbs 17:17

- Proverbs 18:24

- Proverbs 24:26

- Proverbs 27:6

- Proverbs 27:9

- Proverbs 27:10

- Ecclesiastes 4:9–10

- John 15:13

5. God has created his own lists of qualities that he considers important in relationships. Together, read these passages. Which traits would affect friendship? Add them to God's List on the board or pad.

- Matthew 5:3–10

- Romans 12:9–18

- 1 Corinthians 13:4–8

- Galatians 5:22–23

- Ephesians 4:2–3, 32

6. Compare the group's list of friendship qualities to God's list. How are they similar? Different?

7. How might you need to adjust your expectations to be more like God's? What unrealistic expectations will you need to let go of?

8. Share with the group a time when a friend expressed one of the qualities on God's list to you, and how it affected you and your friendship.

9. "The only way to have a friend is to be one," said Ralph Waldo Emerson. You've identified your expectations for friends, but to be a faithful friend in turn, you'll need to develop these qualities yourself. Of all the qualities discussed, what is the one that you need to specifically work on? Why?

10. Romans 12:10 says to "Honor one another above yourselves." Describe a time when you practiced this principle. When you honored your friend, were you still able to meet your needs? Why, or why not?

11. Suppose that this week, you need to lovingly express an expectation to a friend: You think you should spend more time together. Devise a step-by-step plan for managing the conversation.

12. Now create an addendum to the plan. If your friend balks at giving you more time, what is your method for working through your difference in needs and opinions?

Friendship Boosters

1. You've talked about a lot of "serious" qualities about friendship, so now let loose. Describe the funniest or most embarrassing incident that happened while you were with a friend.

2. On a small piece of paper, write your name and the one friendship quality you want to work on developing in yourself. Drop the papers into a bowl, mix them up, and ask each woman to pick a piece of paper. This week, pray for the woman you received in the drawing.

> *The more I experience human intimacy, the more I become aware of its limitations. More and more I realize its inability to satisfy totally the infinite capacity of my heart. Therefore, experiencing the limitations of human intimacy, I long more and more for intimacy with God, whether or not I realize I am longing for him.*
>
> PAUL HINNEBUSCH

Just for Fun

Plan a field trip you can take "just for fun" sometime during the six weeks that your discussion group meets. The goal: to spend time laughing together. You could attend a play, movie, circus, comedy gig, or one-day seminar. Or go bowling, roller blading, canoeing, or horseback riding. Before you decide on the activity, ask group members to express any expectations about the outing. As best you can, incorporate these needs into your decision.

> *By friendship you mean the greatest love, the greatest usefulness, the most open communication.*
>
> JEREMY TAYLOR

Praying Together

Conduct three short rounds of prayer. Ask three volunteers to pray for (1) the women who need new friendships; (2) the ones who need to clarify expectations with current friends; (3) those who want to be better friends. You don't need to admit anything aloud. Just agree silently with the woman who prays for your need.

Making It Real
in Your Own Life

1. Take a few minutes to write out any thoughts about this session that were meaningful or troublesome to you. Ask God to deepen your spiritual insight regarding these matters.

2. Remember the friendship quality you said you wanted to work on (question 9)? Practice it in some way every day this week. You're more likely to remember if you write down a simple plan.

> *One who knows how to show and accept kindness will be a friend better than any possession.*
> SOPHOCLES

Nobody's Just Like You, Thank God!

Opposites attract, but can they stay good friends? Or does friendship depend on having lots of interests and opinions in common?

"One of my great concerns—something I see frequently in Christian circles—is the tendency to isolate ourselves from those who are different from us," says Luci Swindoll. "We gravitate toward people who think like we think, agree with us on everything, believe like we do, even dress the same. In so doing we miss wonderful, God-given opportunities to expand our understanding of the world and the people in it." We also miss out on opportunities to grow personally and spiritually.

So, does this mean all your friends should be notably different than you? Not really. A stimulating mix of friends includes those with similar (ah, isn't it great to hear Mozart together?) and different (she hates cowboy boots and you own three pair) tastes, styles, interests, ethnicity, personalities, and backgrounds.

Of course, midst the diversity you need a soul mate or two—friends you connect with easily and deeply—to anchor the whole rollicking party. But before you shout, "Who's got time for so many people?!" let's clarify what diversity can pack into two or three friendships. Even if your friends resemble casts of thousands, you still need the essentials of depth and quality somewhere in that crowd.

And let's face it. Nobody's just like you. (Thank God! That would be utterly boring.) The greatest examples of sisterhood still have individual differences, but they respect rather than revile, enjoy rather than envy, their friends. They take time to "settle in" with and accept one another, so what seems quirky grows endearing.

For this session you'll talk about how to manage the differences in your friendships so they become assets rather than liabilities. Your model? Jesus, who befriended a fickle group of disciples, plus assorted outcasts and eccentrics—and survived to tell about it!

> *Life is partly what we make it, and partly*
> *it is made by the friends we choose.*
>
> ANONYMOUS

A Moment
for Quiet Reflection

1. What types of friends do you need? Create job descriptions for them. For example:

- The Encourager: encourages and offers hope; sees the best in you.
- The Playmate: loves to have fun and insists that you do, too.
- The Prophet: challenges you to grow spiritually and shore up weaknesses.

Write as many job descriptions as you desire. Which female friends fulfill these "jobs" in your life now? (One person may play several roles.) Which roles are missing, and how could you add them into your circle of friends?

2. In the space below, describe one of your friends who is very different from you. Then list the positives she ushers into your life. Pray for her and the prosperity of your friendship.

Knowing God's Heart

If anybody ever had a diverse group of friends, it was Jesus.

Think about it. There was the passionate and impulsive Simon Peter, the loyal yet hotheaded John, the efficient but bossy Martha, the savvy but sly Zacchaeus, the spiritual and emotional Mary Magdalene. (Just to name a few!) The Master perfected the art of diverse friendships—everything from small stylistic differences to big personality clashes.

Jesus was the ideal friend because he was the flawless man.

"I, however, am pretty flawed," you sigh.

That's okay, so is everyone else. But you can learn from his example and, with the Holy Spirit's help, improve on appreciating how your friends are different from you.

1. In the first session you discussed expectations for friendships. Now let's explore how to accept one another's differences. Can expectations and differences coexist in relationships? Why, or why not?

2. Listed on the following page are six of the twelve disciples who formed Jesus' close circle of friends. They were diverse and demanding, yet devoted to him.

Assign one or more disciple to each woman (a large group can work in pairs), and read the Bible passages. Look for that disciple's initial character traits when he met Jesus and record them below.[1] You don't have to come up with a character trait for each passage. Rather, after you've read the indicated passages, right down your collective, overall understanding of this disciple's character.

If you're pressed for time, only look up the passages marked with an asterisk (*).

Simon Peter: Luke 22:31–34*; Matthew 14:22–31*; John 21:1–19; Matthew 16:13–19*; Acts 2:14*, 37–40

James, son of Zebedee: Matthew 4:18–21; Mark 3:17*; Mark 10:35–40*; Luke 9:52–56*; Acts 12:1–2*

John, son of Zebedee (brother to James): Matthew 4:18–21; Mark 3:17; Mark 10:35–40; Luke 9:52–56*; John 19:26–27*; John 21:20–24*

Andrew (Peter's brother): Matthew 4:18–20*; John 1:35–42; John 6:8–9*

Bartholomew (Nathanael): John 1:45–51*; John 21:1–13

Thomas: John 14:5–6*; John 20:24–29*; John 21:1–13

• Character traits

---

[1]Passages derived from "The Twelve Disciples," *Life Application Bible*, New International Version (Wheaton, IL, and Grand Rapids, MI: Tyndale House Publishers, Inc. and Zondervan Publishing House, 1991), 1734–35.

3. Next, indicate the Lord's response to that disciple. Then note how this disciple changed after three years with Jesus.

- What Jesus said to him

- How the disciple changed

4. Based on the previous passages, name three or more ways Jesus managed his diverse friendships.

5. Did any of his methods surprise you? If so, explain.

6. If you were in Jesus' place, what would you have said to these disciples?

7. What was the outcome of his friendship tactics?

8. What one "friendship method" of the Lord's would help you the most in appreciating the differences between you and a particular friend?

9. Together, decide on the top five ways you can nurture the differences in your friendships.

10. Using this list, discuss how you can respect and nurture the differences in your discussion group.

Friendship Boosters

1. Do you have some fun, secret dreams about being different than you are? Share the answers to these questions with the group. Be free to share outrageous ideas, surprise a few people, and giggle about your "wanna be" fantasies.

   - If you had the talent, what would be your fantasy career? Why?

   - If you could live somebody else's life for one day, whose would it be? Why?

2. Tell your group one of the following:

   - an unusual food combination that you like to eat

   - the most stupid comment you've ever made to someone

   - the goofiest piece of clothing that you like to wear

> *A companion loves some agreeable qualities which a man may possess, but a friend loves the man himself.*
> JAMES BOSWELL

- the most outrageous thing you've done for fun

- what silly thing you'd do if you wouldn't get caught

After the gasps and laughs and looks of surprise, the group can say in unison to each woman, "We love you anyway!"

Just for Fun

Make a date with a friend in the group to share an activity from each other's lives. Each woman should participate in something she doesn't usually do. A young single woman without children could shop for kids' clothes with a married friend. In turn, the mother could attend a college campus function with the single. Or, accommodate both of your music tastes by attending a jazz festival, then a country music concert. Or, try out each other's favorite sport. Be creative!

> *There can be no Friendship where there is no Freedom.*
> WILLIAM PENN

Praying Together

Create a prayer schedule for the week, based on your group's individual needs. For example, "Monday, let's all pray for Janet's exam. Tuesday, we'll pray for Carol's heavy deadline schedule. Wednesday, for a new baby-sitter for Gena." And so forth. Be prepared to report back on progress at the next session. Also pray for one another before you leave today.

Making It Real
in Your Own Life

1. Start a "friend appreciation" journal. Keep track of the things you love about your friends, both their similarities and differences from you. Write down wise, humorous, and meaningful words they say to you. Describe some of your best times together. Paste in photos. Later, for a special occasion—or just because it feels like the right time—share excerpts from the journal with each respective friend.

2. Ask yourself, "Am I aware of anything—a habit or character trait, perhaps—in my life that is driving a friend crazy? What can I do about this?" Then prepare to do it.

Don't bypass the potential for meaningful
relationships just because of differences.
Explore them. Embrace them. Love them.
LUCI SWINDOLL

Hugs and a Good, Swift Kick

*D*o you ever wonder why your bunch of friends got together? Or what attracted you to a particular one-to-one friendship?

You may think it's your good taste, lovely personalities, or knee-slapping humor that decided it. Or the fact you carpool together or exercise on the same nights at the gym. Or maybe it just seemed like an accident.

But what if it was God who brought you together?

"For a Christian, there are, strictly speaking, no 'chances.' A secret Master of Ceremonies has been at work," wrote C. S. Lewis. "Christ, who said to the disciples, 'Ye have not chosen me, but I have chosen you' can say truly to every group of Christian friends, 'You have not chosen one another but I have chosen you for one another.' The friendship is not a reward for our discrimination and good taste in finding one another out.... At *this* feast, it is He who has spread the board and it is He who has chosen the guests. It is He, we may dare to hope, who sometimes does (and always should) preside. Let us not reckon without our Host."[1]

God orchestrating your introductions? That puts a different spin on friendship. Suddenly you feel special, purposeful—and responsible.

---

[1]C. S. Lewis, *The Four Loves* (New York: Harcourt, Brace, Jovanovich, Inc., 1960), 126–27.

If God matched you up, he probably has ideas about what you're to do together. No, this doesn't mean he'll turn you into robots and take away the fun. God wants his children to be joyful, secure, and mature (but this doesn't mean stodgy), and women like that enjoy their lives. He crossed your paths so you can love, support, and challenge one another. Think of it as lots of hugs and occasionally a good, swift kick when you need it.

You'll explore the hugs-and-kick approach to friendship in this session.

Whether you are blessed with soul mates who settle into the most comfortable room inside you, or with those who walk with you just a little while, not one of these people crosses your path by chance.
Each is a messenger, sent by God, to give you the wisdom, companionship, comfort, or challenge you need for a particular leg of your spiritual journey.
TRACI MULLINS

A Moment
for Quiet Reflection

1. Read Psalm 23. It poetically expresses how the Lord cares
for you. In turn, how can you show God's love and support
to a friend in these ways?

- Lying down in green pastures; leading to quiet waters
(verse 2)

- Restoring her soul (verse 3)

- Guiding in paths of righteousness (verse 3)

- Fearing no evil (verse 4)

- Comforting her (verse 4)

- Preparing a table in the presence of enemies (verse 5)

- Anointing her head with oil (verse 5)

- Following her with goodness and love (verse 6)

- Dwelling in the house of the Lord (verse 6)

2. Do you need any Psalm 23 caring in your life? Ask God to
meet your need through a friend this week. Don't be shy
about asking a friend to help you.

Knowing God's Heart

Jesus showed compassion and support to many people. He healed the sick, opened deaf ears and blind eyes, straightened bent limbs, fed the hungry thousands, delivered the demon possessed, and raised the dead.

To begin his ministry, Jesus strolled into the temple, unrolled the prophet Isaiah's scroll, and read: "The Spirit of the Lord is on me, because he has anointed me to preach good news to the poor. He has sent me to proclaim freedom for the prisoners and recovery of sight for the blind, to release the oppressed, to proclaim the year of the Lord's favor" (Luke 4:18–19).

"Today this scripture is fulfilled," said Jesus to the synagogue crowd, referring to himself.

The hometown folks were amazed. "Who is this man who speaks with such gracious words?" they asked. "Isn't he Joseph's son?"

It didn't take long, though, for Jesus to utter honest words that made them angry. So angry, they drove him out of town and tried throwing him off a cliff. He escaped the crowd and proceeded to comfort people and preach for three more years.

Love and truth. Support and honesty. (Hugs and a swift kick.) These were the Lord's hallmarks in relationships.

1. Read together the brief story of Jesus' visit to Mary and Martha's house in Luke 10:38–42. Name three ways Jesus showed his love and support to Mary and Martha.

2. At the same time, when Martha complained to Jesus, he was honest with her about the two women's priorities. So be honest, too. How do you feel about the Lord's response to Martha? Why?

3. How do you think Martha responded to the Lord's words?

4. If you feel comfortable, share a time when a friend challenged you about your priorities and how you responded. Looking back, how do you feel about those challenging words now?

5. We meet Mary and Martha again in John's account of Lazarus's death. Read the beginning of the story in John 11:1–16. Verses 1–3 clearly indicate that Jesus loved this family of sisters and a brother, yet when he heard of Lazarus's illness, he stayed away for two more days. His delay may seem callous, but what was the Lord's purpose for this?

6. How did his return to Bethany prove his love for the grief-stricken family?

7. Now read verses 17–37. How did Jesus show tenderness to both Mary and Martha?

8. How did he challenge each of them?

9. Why would Jesus challenge them during a sorrowful time?

10. What were at least three benefits of Jesus' letting Lazarus die and then participating in the grief process with his sisters?

11. Finish the story in verses 38–45. Aside from the fact that the Father hears his Son, what else does the Lord's prayer reveal about his relationship with God?

12. In the previous lesson you observed Jesus' acceptance of the differences among his friends, how he believed the best for them, and the ways they grew and changed because of his influence. From these two Mary-and-Martha stories, what principles about love/support and truth/honesty in friendships can you learn from Jesus?

13. For many women it's easier to express supportive words than be completely honest. Is that true for you? Why or why not?

14. Why is straightforward communication with a friend often an uneasy task?

15. The Bible says to speak the truth in love so we can "grow up into [Christ]" (Eph. 4:15). How do you earn the right to be candid with a friend about her shortcomings?

16. When you need to be honest, how can you ensure you're speaking the truth in love and not just spewing out whatever comes to mind?

Friendship Boosters

1. Have a compliment fest. Write your first and last name at the top of a piece of paper. Then at the leader's signal, pass the paper to the person sitting at your right. Beneath your name, she will write down a positive trait or compliment about you, while you're doing the same for someone else.

Again at the leader's signal, keep passing the papers to the right, jotting down compliments about the woman whose name appears at the top of each page. Don't duplicate what someone else has written on a page. When you receive your paper back, you're finished. And you'll have a list of wonderful things about yourself!

2. Draw names so you can give a "hug present" to a group member. This gift is something she can hold when you're not there to hug her yourself. Ideas: a small doll, toy, pillow, blanket, picture, locket, gift book, or stuffed animal. It doesn't need to cost much; it's the thought that counts. Bring the gift to next week's session.

Just for Fun

Write a humorous "Truth in Friendship" contract with group members. Include what you will never say and what you will always say. For example: "I will never tell you your hair looks bad. I will always say when you have lettuce bits stuck in your teeth."

> *The best mirror is an old friend.*
> GEORGE HERBERT

Praying Together

Do a round of brief prayers, asking each person to complete this sentence: "Lord, help us to be more loving to our friends by ..."

If time allows, do a second round with the sentence: "Lord, help us to be more truthful to our friends by ..."

> *My friend is he who will tell me my faults in private.*
> ANONYMOUS

Making It Real in Your Own Life

1. Draw a road map of your life. What things have gotten in the way of supportive and honest friendships? This week, create a plan to remove them.

2. Privately select one friend you need to be more truthful with. Pray each day about the opportunity to "speak the truth in love" and grow closer together because of it.

> *We need the help of someone who opens the door wide enough for us to glimpse our real selves. As they lovingly hold us accountable for our actions, words, attitudes, promises, and goals, we gain valuable insight into ourselves.*
> LUCIBEL VANATTA

Putting Your Feet to the Fire

According to Barbara Johnson, you can tell it's going to be a rotten day when you call suicide prevention and they put you on hold; you put your bikini on backwards and it fits better; your blind date turns out to be your ex-boyfriend.

She's joking, of course. But it's serious business when you lose a job, you need surgery, your teenager runs away from home, your husband wants a divorce, a child gets deathly ill, or a parent dies. In times like these, you could definitely use some friends.

From skirmishes at the office to life-shattering news, you need friends who'll listen as your emotions burst, help hold your life together, and not fade away when the difficulties drag on. You need people who commit with a capital C (not to be confused with being controlling or codependent), and even if they live too many miles away for frequent give-a-hug contact, they carry you in their hearts. Then when it's their turn to sob, they need the same from you.

Believe it or not, it's easiest to commit when there's a crisis. The need is obvious. The stakes are high. Everyone notices and rushes in with baked hams and green bean casseroles. Instead, it's the "small stuff" in a friendship that makes your palms sweat and tests your commitment. You argue about politics. She needs a ride to work … again. You haven't paid back that fifty dollars yet. She's in denial about her self-sabotage. You drop by and need to talk when she's really busy. How's your commitment then? Will you stick it out or after enough "little things" pile up, toss aside the friendship like yesterday's newspaper? (Been there, done that, too inconvenient, movin' on.)

It's interesting. You sign a contract for marriage, a license to drive a car, a mortgage to own a house, a W–2 form (yuck) for a job, an agreement to join a health club, a birth certificate for your kids, but there are no documents to bind you to a friendship. No sealed stamp of commitment. No official guidelines … unless you consider God's Word.

For this group meeting you'll talk about commitment in friendship. You'll also study examples of committed friends in the Bible. Maybe you'll be so inspired, you'll run out and do something wonderful for a friend!

True friendship is a plant of slow growth, and must undergo and withstand the shocks of adversity before it is entitled to the appellation.

ABRAHAM LINCOLN

A Moment
for Quiet Reflection

1. Write out how you feel about commitment in friendships. Does it scare you? Why? Have you experienced it? When? Do you know how to extend it? Why or why not? Offer up your questions and concerns to God. Ask him for wisdom as you delve into this topic during the group session.

2. Don't stop there, though. Also recall wonderful acts of commitment from friends. Describe the actions, the emotions, the ways they affected your life. Thank God for them.

Knowing God's Heart

Ever hear the expression "Let your feet do the talking"?

In friendship terms this translates into "Don't just *say* you're my friend. *Show me* by your actions." Sometimes talking with your feet means walking alongside someone, smelling the tulips and grinning a lot. Other times, it means "putting your feet to the fire" and feeling the pain with her.

You may not have thought about it, but the Bible says feet play an important role in relationships. It applauds those whose feet carry good news and peace (Isa. 52:7; Rom. 10:15) and denounces those whose feet run to mischief and destruction (Prov. 6:16, 18; Isa. 59:7, 9). Scripture also unfolds heartwarming stories about friends who talked with their feet in astounding ways. So before letting your feet do the talking, "let your fingers do the walking" through the Scriptures—and meet some remarkably committed friends.

1. Divide in pairs, choose one of the following friendship stories, and read it aloud to each other. What words of commitment did one friend say to another? (If the words aren't stated in the text, imagine what the friends might have said.)

- Ruth's feet followed Naomi back to the homeland (Ruth 1:1–14; 4:9–17).
- Jonathan helped David's feet run toward safety (1 Samuel 20).
- Three friends stuck their feet in the fiery furnace (Daniel 3:4–30).
- Four friends hotfooted a lame man to Jesus (Mark 2:1–12).

2. How did the friend(s) follow up with an act of
commitment?

3. What risk was involved in this act of commitment?

4. How did this commitment express faith in God?

5. What were the outcomes (personal, spiritual, historical) of
this commitment?

6. What would have been the outcome if the friend(s) had avoided commitment?

7. Consider the biblical friends' words of commitment again. If this person wanted to avoid the commitment, what could he or she have said? Express the excuse in today's language. For example, Jonathan could have said, "David, I need you to respect my boundaries. I'm concerned about our becoming too enmeshed in each other's lives."

8. Take turns reporting your biblical friendship stories to the whole group. Explain the dilemma the friends faced, then present your answers to questions 2 and 3. If more than one duo studies a particular story, alternate giving your responses to the questions.

9. What principles about commitment in friendship can you glean from these stories?

10. Share with the group one of the stories about a friend's act of commitment to you from this session's "A Moment of Quiet Reflection."

11. Consider the following words of Patsy Clairmont. What practical questions do they raise about commitment?

"Jesus chose twelve disciples, but he seemed especially close to three of them—Peter, James, and John—and even closer to just one—John, whom he called Beloved. Perhaps this would be a good guide for our friendships.

"I've learned that I can't be best buddies with as many as I'd like because time and life just don't permit it. But twelve dear friends, three of them close, and one of them especially dear . . . I can do that.

"I must remember, though, that my circle of friends are human and will not always be there when I need them. In the Garden of Gethsemane, when Jesus sought out a soft shoulder, he found his disciples in la-la land. Z-z-z. They were too weary to care for anyone but themselves. . . . In our humanness, we sometimes fail one another. This does not negate our need for friendship, but it does remind us to have realistic expectations of people's abilities and availabilities. It also reminds us that there is One who will rush to meet us like the prodigal's parent when he returned home. How can we feel forlorn with the assurance of that kind of joyful reception and warm embrace?"

12. Patsy points to the practical aspects of commitment in friendship. If you and a friend are both stressed-out and overcommitted, how can you be realistic and practical about your friendship and still be committed to one another?

13. What telltale signs would indicate that you and/or a friend have an unhealthy level of commitment to each other?

14. When you see these signs, what can you do?

15. Do you harbor any fears about commitment to a friend? (Not to worry; many of us do.) Tell the group about them, and you'll probably discover that you're not alone. To take the edge off, express your fear as a metaphor: "To me commitment feels like being swallowed up by a big, black sinkhole." Or, "Commitment feels like a whining siren."

16. Use these metaphors to spark some group think: "Why do you (we) crave commitment, but fear it at the same time?" Any suggestions for how you can overcome the fear?

17. Read 1 John 3:18 together. Then write it on a 3 x 5 card, take it home, and keep it as a biblical motto for your friendships.

> *Friends show their love in times of trouble.*
>
> EURIPIDES

Friendship Boosters

1. Share a time when you were in trouble or hardship and a friend bailed you out, comforted you profoundly, or did something sacrificial to help you. How did this act affect you and the situation?

2. Before you leave the session, commit to do one small thing this week for somebody in the group. (Agree together on what it will be.) Mail a letter, run an errand, call her and talk, read a Bible verse to her, water her flower bed. After you fulfill your commitment, notice how you feel. Compare notes on your respective feelings.

> *A friend is a person with whom I may be sincere.*
> *Before him I can think aloud.*
>
> RALPH WALDO EMERSON

Just for Fun

As a group, write a humorous list called, "You know you're committed to a friend when . . ." Here are a few starters:

- All of her Tupperware® now resides at your house.
- Your kids now call her Mom. (She cooks homemade meals.)
- She says, "You don't look fat," before you have to ask.
- She's survived five different boyfriends with you.

Praying Together

As a benediction to this session, read aloud Psalm 20:1–7, as a prayer of blessing and commitment to your group:

May the LORD answer you when you are in distress; may the name of the God of Jacob protect you. May he send you help from the sanctuary and grant you support from Zion. May he remember all your sacrifices and accept your burnt offerings. May he give you the desire of your heart and make all your plans succeed. We will shout for joy when you are victorious and will lift up our banners in the name of our God. May the LORD grant all your requests. Now I know that the LORD saves his anointed; he answers him from his holy heaven with the saving power of his right hand. Some trust in chariots and some in horses, but we trust in the name of the LORD our God.

Making It Real in Your Own Life

1. Take a meal—complete with candles, silver stemware, cloth napkins, the works—to a struggling friend. (It doesn't have to be expensive food. A hamburger on a delicate china pattern could make you giggle.) Stay for conversation.

2. Pull out photos of friends and place them together on your bedroom bureau. Then as you dress for the day, say prayers of commitment and blessing for each person.

A true friend is someone who thinks that you are a good egg even though he knows you are slightly cracked.
BERNARD MELTZER

Friendship Flops
and Fizzles

Patsy Clairmont says there are twelve ways to insure a small repertoire of friends. Here's her list for surefire ways to remain lonely:

1. Breed pettiness.
2. Campaign against your friend's mate.
3. Drop in frequently.
4. Offer unsolicited advice.
5. Create opportunities to whine.
6. Nitpick her children.
7. Besiege her with phone calls.
8. Critique her decisions.
9. Encourage dissensions.
10. Share freely in all her possessions.
11. Snub her other friends.
12. Insist on being her best friend.

Every woman could create her own list, couldn't she? There are plenty of ways to get under each other's skin, and if we're not careful, the joy of friendship can be reduced to pettiness. But who wants that? If we admire someone enough to be her friend, we'd like for the relationship to continue, right? And that means swiftly dealing with your failures, disappointments, and misunderstandings.

In this session you'll discuss how to truly love one another through these episodes. You'll also stretch to form a biblical response to friendships that flop because of conflict or fizzle out for lack of interest. The goal? To deepen your intimacy, strengthen your bonds, and make relationships last.

> *To know someone here or there with whom you can feel*
> *there is understanding in spite of distances or thoughts*
> *expressed—that can make life a garden.*
>
> GOETHE

A Moment
for Quiet Reflection

1. In stream-of-consciousness fashion, for five minutes write out everything that the word "love" means to you. Don't censor yourself, think something through, or edit what you write.

2. A day later, read your descriptions. Is there a theme that emerges? If so, in a sentence, define what love means to you. How has this definition affected your friendships?

Knowing God's Heart

Love, love, love. That's the Bible's redemptive message. God loves you and shook the earth to prove it. He wants you to love him. He asks you to love others.

When people think of love, it's hearts and flowers. But when God defines love, it's a hand-to-the-plow-and-don't-look-back kind of perseverance. A belief that gets its hands dirty to pull out the best in another person. A hope that forgives.

It's pretty hard to spread around this kind of love, unless you're connected to the Lover of your soul. So once again, it's back to the Scriptures to compare humanity's limited love to his boundless supply . . .

1. According to John 13:34, as God's children, why are we to love others?

2. How are we to express this love?

- Romans 12:9

- 1 Peter 1:22

3. What enables us to love our friends and others?

- Romans 5:5

- 2 Corinthians 5:14–15

4. What does John 14:21 give as the benefits of keeping God's commandment to love one another?

5. How can "loving as God loved us" play out in friendships? Look up the verses below and write the answers under the column, "God's Way." (You will complete the column, "Human Way," in the next question.)

	God's Way	*Human Way*
• Matthew 5:44		
• Galatians 5:13		
• Ephesians 4:2		
• Ephesians 4:14–15		
• Philippians 2:2		
• Colossians 3:13		
• 1 John 3:16		
• 1 John 3:18		

6. God's kind of loving is radically different than the natural human response. Next to each entry under "God's Way" to love, jot down the way humans are tempted to respond when wronged or upset. For example, Matthew 5:44 says we're to love our enemies and pray for them. The human response is to hate our enemies and seek revenge on them.

7. If you were in the middle of a misunderstanding with a friend, which of the previous verses would be the most helpful to you (to give you God's perspective)? What would be a biblical motivation for resolving your problems?

8. Considering the previous verses and Matthew 18:21–35, how would you resolve these conflicts with a friend?

- Things she does that irritate you

- Words she said that hurt you

- A sin she committed against you

9. The Bible doesn't say you're to be close friends with everybody. What limitations are Christians encouraged to make?

- Psalm 1:1

- Matthew 8:15–18

- 2 Corinthians 6:14–17

- Galatians 6:1

10. In light of the previous passages, what would you do in these cases?

- A friend is habitually sinning, without remorse.

- She has forsaken God altogether.

- She asks you to participate in sin.

11. Jesus befriended sinners. Read one of those instances in Matthew 9:10–13. What was Jesus' reply when the Pharisees questioned him about eating with tax collectors and sinners?

12. Does his response contradict Psalm 1:1? Why or why not?

13. Name one specific way these passages can guide your relationships with non-Christians.

14. Would it be biblical to forsake a friendship simply because you're not interested in the person, don't have much in common, or have drifted apart? If you say yes, what would be a loving way to end the friendship? If you say no, how would you handle the relationship?

15. What would be a biblical response if a friend rejects her friendship with you?

16. Think of a friendship you're having difficulty with. What concept from this lesson can you apply to that friendship?

> *True friendship is like sound health; the value of it is seldom known until it be lost.*
>
> CHARLES CALEB COLTON

Friendship Boosters

1. Conduct a fun "awards ceremony" for the commitments that group members have made to friends. Give a silly gift to the person who

- has the longest friendship with another woman.
- took the longest vacation with a friend.
- loaned the most money to a friend and kept the friend.
- had the longest phone conversation with a friend.
- spent the most consecutive hours baby-sitting for a friend.

2. Even if it's not February, make Valentine cards for your friends, saying how much you love and appreciate them. Hand deliver the ones you can. Mail the others. The responses might be fun and funny.

Just for Fun

Go out to lunch or dinner together and call it a love feast. Pay for somebody's dinner and let someone pay for yours. Talk about the people you love, and what you love about each other.

Praying Together

Ask four woman to pray on behalf of the struggling and broken friendships in your group. The first woman should say a prayer of *thanksgiving* for these friendships. The second, a prayer of *repentance* for the sins committed in these friendships. The third, a *petition* for help and wisdom. The fourth, *intercession* for the friends in these relationships.

> *Be slow to fall into friendship; but when thou art in,*
> *continue firm and constant.*
>
> SOCRATES

Making It Real
in Your Own Life

1. To soak the meaning of love into your soul, read 1 Corinthians 13 every day this week.

2. Take a forgiveness walk. Choose a setting you enjoy and think of a friend you need to forgive. As you walk through the area, at various landmarks stop briefly and forgive that friend for what she did to you. Then as you leave, believe that you've tossed away the offenses and truly forgiven her.

If you judge people, you have no time to love them.

MOTHER TERESA

Come On, Get Happy!

You and a friend work at the same company. She receives a whopper of a promotion. Much more pay. A bigger benefits package. More travel (which she wants). Executive status. Power.

You've been slaving away at the same thankless job for five years.

What do you do?

a. Avoid talking to her and begin downsizing the friendship.
b. Say you're happy for her, but emphasize how hard her job will be.
c. Congratulate her, but go home and rail at God.
d. Throw a party for her at your expense, not expecting anything in return.

Real friendship—a satisfying, life-giving companionship—supports each other through the valleys, but also races to the mountaintop and shouts "Hallelujah!" when one of you fulfills a desire or meets success. You don't wait until *both* of you hit a windfall before you jump for joy. You take turns hitting the high spots, but celebrate together. (Not a bad way to go. You didn't do anything noteworthy, but you still get to party!)

In the midst of life's "stuff," friends need to celebrate. But you don't have to wait for a significant event or obvious reason to get happy. You can create "joy breaks" along the way. Take it from friends Marilyn Meberg and Luci Swindoll. The unexpected and spontaneous does a friendship good.

"Yesterday I wandered into my kitchen at 6:30 A.M. to activate my 'Mrs. Tea' and noticed a human being sitting on my patio reading the paper," recalls Marilyn. "I stopped dead in my tracks and then realized it was Luci. I threw open the slider door. 'Hey, early bird, what are you doing nesting on my patio at 6:30 in the morning?' I asked.

"She looked up at me with a smile. 'You wanna go out for breakfast?'

"I rapidly thought through my tightly scheduled day. . . . Going out for breakfast would definitely throw off my timing, but then Luci and I had just recently become neighbors. It's the first time in twelve years we've lived anywhere near each other. How nice to take time to enjoy her nearness. 'Okay, let's go.'

"Moments later, we were chortling over the world's finest cinnamon rolls. As I sat down at my desk an hour and a half later than I had planned, I felt only joy for the spontaneous intrusion into my well-ordered day. It was a no-big-deal experience, but by the same token it was softly pleasant and soul satisfying. Also, I always enjoy a good cinnamon roll."

During this session you'll consider how to infuse "joy breaks" into your friendships, too.

> *Anybody can sympathize with the suffering*
> *of a friend, but it requires a very fine nature to*
> *sympathize with a friend's success.*
> OSCAR WILDE

A Moment
for Quiet Reflection

1. Do you have joy breaks with the friends in your life? On a scale of one to ten, rate yourself: 10 = "I'm bubbling with joy and spontaneity"; 1 = "Joy? What's joy?" Brainstorm how you can introduce more small celebrations into your friendships.

2. How about your relationship with God? Are you taking joy breaks with him? Again, dream up ways you can celebrate your imaginative Creator. Then take a joy break right now. Read the following passage, Psalm 150, to the Lord. Then once more, with feeling.

> *Praise the LORD. Praise God in his sanctuary;*
> *praise him in his mighty heavens.*
> *Praise him for his acts of power;*
> *praise him for his surpassing greatness.*
> *Praise him with the sounding of the trumpet,*
> *praise him with the harp and lyre,*
> *Praise him with tambourine and dancing,*
> *praise him with the strings and flute,*
> *Praise him with the clash of cymbals,*
> *praise him with resounding cymbals.*
> *Let everything that has breath praise the LORD.*
> *Praise the LORD.*

Finish off your joy break by singing a God-praising hymn.

Knowing God's Heart

1. When the angel told Mary she'd conceive and become Christ's mother, without delay she celebrated with a friend. Read her story in Luke 1:26–56. What could have kept Mary from sharing her good news with Elizabeth?

2. What kind of woman must Elizabeth have been to respond to Mary with joy? Name several character traits.

3. To whom do you immediately tell your good news? Explain why you tend to tell this person first.

4. Mary's song to the Lord is a mini history lesson about God's goodness to his people. What do her poetic words tell you about the Lord's character?

5. Why do you think Mary chose to emphasize these traits in the midst of her celebration?

6. Elizabeth celebrated with Mary out of sheer joy and expectation. Sometimes when people celebrate with you (or you with them), it is an act of forgiveness. Read the parable of the prodigal son in Luke 15:11–32. What feelings and offenses did the father need to forgive so he could celebrate his son's return?

7. The father lept over the offenses he could have used to punish his son. What would have prepared his heart to do so?

8. Unfortunately, when you have good news, not everybody feels celebratory. What was an obvious reason the older son grumbled about his brother's party? What could have been the not-so-obvious reasons?

9. If you were getting that big job promotion, and your friend bursts into tears because she's been passed over, what could you do?

10. In what specific ways can you be sure you don't play the grumbling brother's role when a friend in your life receives mercy and goodness—and it seems like she doesn't deserve it?

11. What about the friend who was "born with a silver spoon in her mouth"? She gets all the breaks and the good things she wants out of life. (Or at least it appears that way.) Name two things you could do to celebrate with her, even if you're down in the dumps.

12. In the following Scripture passages, discover the other ways God asks us to take joy breaks or celebrate together. Why would these be important elements in our friendships?

- Ecclesiastes 3:1, 4; Romans 12:15

- Psalm 118:1

- Psalm 119:16

- Proverbs 15:15

- Ephesians 5:19–20

- 1 Thessalonians 5:17–18

- 1 Peter 4:9

- Hebrews 10:25

13. In practical terms, how can you integrate these biblical joy breaks and celebrations into your friendships? Choose two actions and discuss how to apply them to your closest friendship.

Friendship Boosters

1. Divide into two teams, leaving one person to act as referee. Play a game of charades in which somebody on one team silently acts out a possible way to take a joy break. (All ideas must be presented to the referee before they are acted out.) If the other team responds correctly, it gets a point. The first team with five points wins the game.

2. Take a joy break together. Cut short your meeting time and go window-shopping, to a movie, or to a coffee shop.

Just for Fun

Throw a "we're done with the Bible study" potluck party. Invite everyone from the group, plus their families. At some point, share a few highlights of what you learned from the study with the nongroup members.

> *Friendship makes prosperity more brilliant, and lightens adversity by dividing and sharing it.*
>
> CICERO

Praying Together

This is the last session of the study, so be a bit ceremonial. For a good send-off, form a circle and hold hands. Each woman can pray aloud for the woman to her left, asking God for a specific "friendship blessing" in her life. ("Lord, for Jean I ask for the blessing of a listening friend as she passes through her son's teenage years." "God, even though Donna's workload is heavy, bless her with friends who encourage her to play.") At the end of each brief prayer, the group can agree by saying, "Amen!"

> *What is a friend? A single soul in two bodies.*
>
> ARISTOTLE

Making It Real
in Your Own Life

1. Write out all of the things worth celebrating in your life. Choose one of those things and ask a friend to celebrate it with you, "for no reason at all."

2. Purchase a book like *Joy Breaks, 31 Days of Praise,* or another title that encourages you to focus on what's good and celebratory in your life. In the next month, read the book and begin putting its praise and appreciation principles into practice.

> *My father used to say that when you die, if you've got five real friends, then you've had a good life.*
> LEE IACOCCA

LEADER'S GUIDE

LESSON ONE

1. Be sure there is a chalkboard or easel and pad available for this lesson, also chalk or marking pens.

2. The answers will vary, so guide the women in talking about the healthy expectations for friendship (need for companionship; someone to give to; a way to have fun, and so forth), and also perhaps some unhealthy expectations (trying to plug a hole inside that only God can fill; someone to do what I need done; a person to take care of my emotional wounds, and so forth). Also, don't try to make the women express what you feel are the "right" or Christian expectations. Encourage them to be honest about their true feelings.

3. You may want to set a timer for ten minutes to decide on this list, or the discussion may swallow up much of your time together.

4. These answers are based on the New International Version of the Bible. Because women in the group may bring varying versions of the Bible, the answers may not always be clear to a woman using a different translation than the NIV. So here is help for determining the answers.
   - Proverbs 17:17: love
   - Proverbs 18:24: loyalty
   - Proverbs 24:26: honesty
   - Proverbs 27:6: trust (some translations may suggest faithfulness)
   - Proverbs 27:9: counsel
   - Proverbs 27:10: longevity (don't forsake your father's friend)
   - Ecclesiastes 4:9–10: help
   - John 15:13: sacrifice

5. Again, these answers may vary, but here are suggestions based on the NIV. If a quality is repeated, it's listed only once.
   - Matthew 5:3–10: perhaps all of these traits, but especially poor in spirit, meek, merciful, pure, peacemaker
   - Romans 12:9–18: love, sincerity, clinging to good, devotion, honor, zealous, spiritual fervor, service, joy, hope, patience, faithfulness, hospitality, blessings, rejoicing, harmony, humility, not revengeful, right living, inner peace
   - 1 Corinthians 13:4–8: kind, not envious, not boastful, not rude, not self-seeking, not angry, doesn't keep record of wrongs, truthful, protects, trusts, perseveres, never fails
   - Galatians 5:22–23: goodness, gentleness, self-control
   - Ephesians 4:2–3, 32: promotes unity, compassionate, forgiving

Friendship Boosters. Idea 2: To keep the session moving, bring the bowl and small pieces of paper to the meeting.

Just for Fun. As the group discusses ideas for the field trip, be sure everyone gets to give input. Especially solicit ideas and expectations from the quieter group members.

LESSON TWO

2–3. If a group needs help synthesizing the passages, these answers can help you coach its members.

Character traits:

- Simon Peter: impulsive, passionate, fearful
- James: ambitious, short-tempered, judgmental, self-righteous
- John: ambitious, judgmental, self-righteous
- Andrew: eager to please
- Bartholomew: doubtful, honest, straightforward
- Thomas: doubtful.

What Jesus said about them:

- Simon Peter: Satan had sifted him; would deny Jesus; had little faith; would glorify God through his death; would be the rock on which Jesus built his church; he would have the keys to the kingdom
- James: called him one of the "Sons of Thunder"; would become a fisher of men; would drink the cup Jesus drank (death by sword)
- John called him one of the "Sons of Thunder"; would become a fisher of men; would drink the cup Jesus drank
- Andrew: would become a fisher of men
- Bartholomew: called him a "true Israelite"; a man who is not false
- Thomas: because he believed, would see Jesus after the resurrection.

How they changed:

- Simon Peter moved from fear to boldness
- James became committed enough to die for the sake of Christ
- John moved from judgmental to loving
- Andrew became someone who told others about Christ
- Bartholomew turned from doubt to belief
- Thomas turned from doubt to belief and courage.

4. There will be many creative answers, but don't miss the point that Jesus believed in who his friends could be, told them so, and stuck with them until they overcame their faults.

7. Again, there may be several answers, but if it isn't mentioned, point out that Jesus' "friendship tactics" caused people to change for the better.

Just for Fun. Be sure that every group member has a partner for this activity. Suggest that sometime during the next four weeks, group members bring in and share from their friendship appreciation journals.

Praying Together. So everyone has a copy, ask each woman to write down the schedule in her notes as it's created.

LESSON THREE

1. Possible answers: Jesus was their friend. He accepted their hospitality. He stayed and taught people in their home. He was close to them, in that Martha felt comfortable to complain to Jesus about Mary's behavior.

5. By delaying his return, Jesus would ultimately fulfill God's purpose and bring glory to him.

6. Returning to Judea, Jesus faced possibly being murdered by his enemies there. But he risked this to see his beloved friends.

7. To comfort her immediately, Jesus told Martha her brother would rise again. He called for Mary and felt troubled when he saw her grief. He wept for Lazarus.

8. Jesus asked Martha, "Do you believe I am the resurrection and the life?" He didn't really even acknowledge either sister's statement, "If you'd come sooner, this wouldn't have happened."

9. Jesus wanted to increase their faith. He knew of the miracle to come.

10. Jesus would create a miracle that would increase their faith. Also, it would increase the faith of the people around them. He would express his love for the sisters by grieving with them. He would show his great love for them by raising Lazarus from the dead. Some might say Jesus showed his love for Lazarus by raising him from the dead.

11. There is deep intimacy between the Father and Son. Jesus is obedient to the Father's will, no matter how much friends pressure him.

12. Possible answers: Loving people means being truthful to them. Honesty can lead to "a greater good" such as personal change, increased faith, and spiritual growth.

   Friendship Boosters. Idea 1: For uniformity and efficiency, you may want to supply the papers, with their names already written on the top. Idea 2: Be sure each woman is included in the name exchange. Also, set a limit on how much a gift could cost, such as under five dollars.

   Just for Fun. Keep a chalkboard or easel and pad available for this activity.

LESSON FOUR

1. When the women divide into pairs, be sure all of the Scripture passages get selected. It's okay if a passage is used by more than one group.

8. Encourage the women to keep their reports concise. You may want to pull out the timer for this question, giving each duo a limit on how long they can talk.

9. Possible answers: Commitment to friends eventually pays off. When we act with commitment, it may take awhile to see the long-term effects. Commitment stretches our faith. Commitment to friends reaps personal rewards.

11. Possible answers: If we're both very busy, how do we stay committed? Practically speaking, how many friends can one person commit to? Do you have to be in physical proximity to be committed in friendship? How do you allow room for failure in friendships?

13. Possible answers: Deceit, jealousy, pent-up anger, being controlling, constant phone calls, incessant caretaking (and the friend is not ill or in crisis), frequent criticizing or putting the other person down, passive-aggressive behavior, expecting to see each other every day, one friend does most of the giving and the other most of the receiving, frequently obsessing about what the other person has said or done.

14. Possible answers: Set healthy boundaries; have an honest but loving confrontation; discuss your differences in expectations and develop a win-win solution; get therapy for yourself; set goals about how to change the negative behavior; pray. In some cases, you may have to terminate the relationship.

17. Bring enough 3 x 5 cards to this session for everyone in the group.

Friendship Boosters. Idea 2: Again, make sure every woman in the group gets to participate.

Just for Fun. Write the answers to this activity on the chalkboard or easel.

LESSON FIVE

Questions 5 & 6: God's way and possible human ways (answers will vary) are:

- Matthew 5:44: love enemies and pray for them/hate your enemies and seek revenge
- Galatians 5:13: serve one another in love/try to seek power or control
- Ephesians 4:2: humble, gentle, patient/proud, harsh, impatient
- Ephesians 4:14–15: speak truth in love/lie or talk behind each other's back
- Philippians 2:2: like-minded in purpose/argue, stir up conflict, sabotage one another
- Colossians 3:13: be forbearing and forgiving/keep track of offenses and hold grudges

- 1 John 3:16: lay down your life/protect your own interests and run when "the going gets tough"
- 1 John 3:18: love with actions and truth/be "all talk and no action" and make excuses for yourself

12. Considering Jesus' actions and Psalm 1:1, the core idea is to befriend and have compassion for nonbelievers without participating in their sin and attitudes. We can't just abandon non-Christians; we are to be a spiritual light to them (Matt. 5:14–16).

Friendship Boosters. Idea 1: Gather up inexpensive gifts for the winners. Use things you already have around the house. For example, the longest friendship could receive a few Geritol® tablets; the longest vacation, a pair of earplugs; loaned the most money, a plastic water gun; longest phone conversation, balm for chapped lips; longest baby-sitting, some aspirin. Idea 2: Bring colors, paper, scissors, paste, glitter, or anything else that would make creative Valentine cards. Or before the meeting, call group members and assign them something to bring to the session.

LESSON SIX

1. Possible answers: Mary could have been ashamed, afraid of what Joseph or Elizabeth or other relatives would think. She may have thought Elizabeth was "too old" to be a meaningful friend. She could have doubted what the angel told her.

2. Possible answers: She believed her friend's words. Elizabeth must have been a woman of great faith, familiar with the Scriptures. She was emotionally mature enough to set aside her pregnancy to celebrate Mary's with her. She was loving and tender to a young girl, whom she could have sloughed off as immature.

5. Mary needed to know that, just as God had been faithful in the past, he would be faithful to her now.

6. Possible answers: The father had to overcome his son's foolishness, rejection, and unloving behavior. He also needed to forsake anger, acting hurt, unforgiveness, and saying "I told you so."

7. Possible answers: The father nurtured his love for the son, so it stayed greater than any offense. He never rejected the prodigal. He may have prayed constantly for him. He'd already decided to forgive his son. He kept hope in his heart.

8. The obvious reasons could possibly be long-term jealousy, past conflicts between the brothers, not feeling secure in his father's love, having been criticized about his work, a revengeful personality.